HOW TO
Make Candles

HOW TO
Make
Candles

A practical step-by-step guide to making beautiful candles

LESLEY SPARKS

NEW HOLLAND

Contents

INTRODUCTION

It is my intention to de-mystify the process of aromatic candle-making and to provide a number of projects to enable the crafter to try their hand at a variety of different candle-making techniques. While the projects shown here focus on natural looking and smelling candles, once the basic techniques have been mastered there is nothing to stop you from experimenting with colour, different types of wax and fragrances.

I attempted to make my first when I was around ten years old, after my father had bought me a candle-making kit. A paraffin wax castle was my first project, but sadly the wax leaked out of the mould and poured onto the kitchen worktop, cupboards and tiled floor, for which I was scolded by my mother. However, a love of candlelight was none-the-less born! Today, I run a small family business, focusing on making candles with a purpose, as well as those with fantastic aromas – the business now supplies a selection of shops and museums and the products are now sold online, and at larger local fairs and events. While I love getting out and meeting people when taking parts in events, the fun part is always the formulating of different mixes of wax and the blending, concocting and research that goes into new aromas.

To my absolute delight, I recently discovered that candle-making was a family trait. My daughter had been asked to do a school project concerning 'an interesting member of your family'. Knowing that my uncle had undertaken some research into our family history, we asked him to email anything that he thought may be of interest and so we discovered that my great, great, great Grandfather Tomas Bohlen, was a chandler (candle-maker) born in Denmark, who later moved to the UK where he patented a process involving stearic acid use in candles. So, it seems being a chandler is in the genes!

CANDLES: FROM ESSENTIAL LIGHT SOURCE TO LUXURY ITEM

Candles in one shape or another have been used by humans for thousands of years, with different nations developing their own forms of light. There is early evidence of candles in Ancient Egypt where rush lights were soaked in molten tallow (a type of animal fat). There are also early records of the Chinese using whale fat and a suggestion that beeswax may have been used at this time.

The Romans introduced a wicked tallow candle using a kind of rush, as opposed to the former more widespread use of the rush lights, which were simply soaked in tallow. Beeswax became more widely used for candles in the Middle Ages, but they were expensive to produce and so tended to be limited to religious houses, royalty and those in higher levels of society.

During the 18th century spermaceti wax was introduced for candle-making, a by-product of the whaling industry – this used wax from the whale head and produced a clean, bright light that rivalled beeswax and was cheaper because of its plentiful supply. The 19th century saw the introduction of paraffin wax, making candles far more affordable to all and the refinement of stearic acid, a fatty acid found in animal and vegetable fat, which could be used alone or, more often, as an addition to paraffin wax increased the burn time of the candles.

In recent years all sorts of waxes and combinations of waxes have been introduced for use in candle-making with soy wax and rapeseed both popular choices.

WAXES FOR CANDLE MAKING

Beeswax
Made in the hives of the honey bee, beeswax has a relatively high melting point of 62–66°C (143–151°F) – this creates a slower burn but also a clean, bright light.

Soy wax
Made from soy beans, soy wax melts at around 50–54°C (122–129°F) and has a slow burn rate in comparison with paraffin wax. There are two main different types of soy wax in current use, a pillar blend for use in making tapers and pillar candles and a container blend for use in making any candle contained within a receptacle, meaning a tin or glass.

Rapeseed wax
Made from hydrogenated rapeseed oil, rapeseed wax has similar properties to soy wax. It is sometimes used in combination with soy wax and can enhance the fragrance of the candle.

Palm wax or carnauba wax
This hard wax with a high melting point is sometimes added to other waxes to harden and increase the burn time.

Stearine wax
Derived from a variety of sources such as fish oils, beef oils, coconut oils and palm nuts, stearine wax is used primarily to harden other waxes and increase the burn time.

Paraffin or mineral wax
Made by the distillation of coal and crude petroleum, paraffin or mineral wax melts at around 56–58°C (133–136°F) and burns with a bright, clean light.

EQUIPMENT AND MATERIALS

YOU WILL NEED

- A heat source
- A double boiler : Either a heatproof glass jug (pitcher) placed inside a large saucepan; two saucepans purpose-made for candle making; and for smaller amounts, a preserving can (tin) and heavy-based baking tray
- A couple of heatproof glass measuring jugs (pitchers) or beakers
- Glass stirring rods or wooden spills (like those supplied in some cafés)
- Spills (wooden splints / coffee stirrers) and elastic bands to make up splints to hold the wick in place
- Measuring scales
- Modeling putty
- An old wooden chopping board
- Glass candle containers – make sure they are specifically made for use as a candle container
- Aluminium tins with a capacity of 50 ml (2 fl oz), 125 ml (4 fl oz), 200ml (7fl oz) and 250ml (8fl oz)
- Taper moulds
- Suitable size wick
- Metal sustainers to hold wick in place
- Wax
- Wax glue to hold the sustainer in position
- Essential or fragrance oils
- Pipettes with measures in ml/fl oz marked on the side

BASIC TECHNIQUES

1. Cover surfaces

Cover your work station with newspaper, a plastic mat or an old oil cloth to protect it from spillages. Have an old chopping board or heat-resistant mat on your table so that you have a safe place to put the receptacle holding hot wax when it is removed from the double boiler.

2. Weighing out the wax

There are various ways of weighing out wax, but the rule of thumb is that the weight of wax in grams is equivalent in millilitres, so 200 g (7 oz) soy wax is around 200 ml (7 fl oz) of wax. Conveniently a 400 ml (14 oz) can holds 200 g (7 oz) wax, which melts to produce 200 ml (7 fl oz) liquid wax. Often with candle-making, you can measure everything with a tin can!

When making container candles or using moulds, the supplier of the container should state how much wax is needed. Otherwise, fill the mould or container with water, then tip this into a measuring beaker to find out how many millilitres or fluid ounces the container or mould holds. Convert this to grams or ounces and weigh it out on your scales. Most modern digital scales will convert this for you.

3. Wick sizes

Some suppliers will have tables on their website with recommendations as to suitable wick sizes for the diameter of candle, the type of wax and whether to use a fragrance oil or not. If the wicks are slightly more expensive but come with sound advice, you will save money in the long run. Once you are happy that the wick works for you, then you will start to become familiar with the sizing of that particular brand. I use a multi-purpose flat-braided, unbleached wick for containers and a square-braided wick for beeswax pillars and tapers.

4. Calculating the essential oils

It is good practice to have essential oils ready before you start melting the candle wax. This is because you need to have your eyes on the wax at all times when it is melting. If maths is not your strong point, then make it easier for yourself by making sure that your container that you are choosing to use to hold your candle is similar in size to the one in the recipe. If it is smaller than the one in the recipe, then you can use any excess mixture to make up some tealights. Just remember, when ordering your wax, to order some tealight holders and wicks, too. In which case you can skip the rest of this and go straight to stage 5!

It is generally recommended that you add between 3 and 9 per cent of essential oils to the total volume of wax. To make things easy the recipes are at 5 per cent:

Container size: 160 g (5½ oz)

Wax: 160 ml (5½ fl oz)
Essential oil blend: 8 ml (160 drops)

Container size: 225 g (8 oz)
Wax: 225ml (8fl oz)
Essential oil blend 11 ml (220 drops)

As an approximate guide, 20 drops of essential oils equal 1 millilitre. This will depend on the viscosity of the oil and the size of drop, but this is a safe guide. To work out the correct percentage of millilitres (and drops) to use when altering a recipe, calculate as follows:

The mosquito candle tin requires 125 ml (4½ fl oz) wax and 7 ml (5 per cent) of oils. So, let's say that you want to make this candle recipe in a 200 ml (7 fl oz) container; in order to use the same ratio of essentials oils, you need to work out the percentage of each oil used. The original recipe requires you to use 1.5 ml lemongrass, 1.5 ml rosemary and 4 ml of citronella, so to work out the percentage of each oil to use, the calculation will look like this:

Rosemary – 1.5 ml ÷ 7, then x 100 = 21 per cent
Lemongrass – 1.5 ml ÷ 7, then x 100 = 21 per cent
Citronella – 4 ml ÷ 7, them x 100 = 57 per cent

In the larger container you would require 10 ml (5 per cent) of essential oils, so now the percentages look like this:

Rosemary – 21 per cent of 10 ml = 2.1 ml
Lemongrass – 21 per cent of 10 ml = 2.1 ml
Citronella – 57 per cent of 10 ml = 5.7 ml

5. Mixing the essential oils

Mix essential oils in a separate little container or beaker, because if you are use a dropper the drops can come out too quickly. This gives you the opportunity to correct any mistakes. If you have too much oil you can always store it in an essential oil bottle or container with a lid. Oils are expensive so don't waste them!

6. Preparing the mould or container

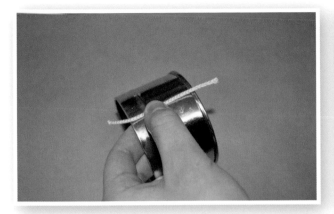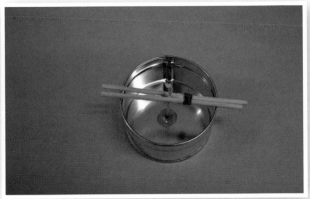

Cut your wick to length by measuring the height of the container or mould and allowing an extra 30 mm (1¼ in) – this allows for a knot at the base and space to put a splint at the top. Knot one end of the wick, thread this through the sustainer and glue it in position with wax glue. (Wax glue is worth tracking down and is much easier to use than sticky tabs.) Once stuck to the base of the container, pull the wick gently so that it is taut and straight and then fix it into place using a splint. You should only need one elastic band, although some people like to use one at each end to make it more secure. If the splints don't stay in the position you want, use some modelling putty.

7. Method for melting the wax

1. Pour a kettle of boiling water into the base of the double boiler or baking tray. Weigh the required amount of wax, and tip it into the second saucepan or heatproof jug (pitcher). Put the receptacle holding the wax into the water.
2. Turn on the heat source and allow the wax to melt, stirring it occasionally with the spill.
3. When the wax has melted, turn off your heat sand using oven gloves (mitts), pour the wax into a mixing jug to which the pre-blended essentials will be added. This method ensures it is the heat from the water that is melting the wax, not the direct heat from a flame or electric heat source.

8. The do's and don'ts of melting wax
- If using a baking tray as the base of the double boiler, make sure that sides are at least 3 cm (1¼ in) tall to contain the water.
- Make sure that the water does not run dry while the wax is melting.
- Jugs (pitchers) and pans will be useful when working with larger quantities of wax.
- The 200 g (7 oz) tin can method is an easy one to use for smaller projects and if you want to keep the quantities simple, a 400 g (14 oz) tin can will contain roughly 200 g (7 oz) of wax.
- Don't use a tin can larger than 400 g (14 oz) – it gets too hot and is unmanageable!
- Remember that the jug (pitcher) or pan handle and the tin can will be hot, so use oven gloves (mitts) or a dish towel to remove containers from the heat source. The golden rule is to turn the heat source OFF before you remove your receptacle.
- Always melt the wax in a separate jug (pitcher) to the one in which you mix the oils. It is really easy to misjudge how much wax you have melted, so by doing this you can get an accurate measurement of the liquid wax that you need, which is really important for calculating how much essential oil to use. If you have leftover wax in your double boiler jug, you can simply let this solidify and cool down, then place it in the refrigerator for 15 minutes and then chip it out and re-use it.
- It is recommended that you use a thermometer to test when your wax is at the pour stage and follow the advice given by your wax supplier. However, there are many other things that can affect the way that a candle sets, such as room temperature, wax temperature and container or mould temperature.
- Allow your containers to be at room temperature for a couple of hours prior to pouring (so do not bring them from a cold storage room and pour the wax straight in!). Make sure the room you are working in is at a comfortable temperature, so if you are in a warm climate, work in a cool room and if you are in a cool climate, work in a warm room. The more you practise, the easier it will become to judge how to manage your own environment.

9. Adding the essential oils
Once you have poured the wax into your pouring jug (pitcher) just after it has all melted, allow it to stand for a couple of seconds before putting in your essential oils – this will minimize the evaporation of the precious oils.

10. Pouring the blend

Once poured, allow the wax mixture to set for 24 hours before using and try not to move or disturb the wax while it is setting. When making candles in moulds, spray some mould release into the mould before you add the wick. If you are having real difficulty releasing the candle from the mould, place it in the freezer for half an hour.

In summary:
1. Weigh the wax.
2. Cut the wick to size and prepare the mould or container ready to receive the wax.
3. Calculate the amount of essential oils required and pour them into a small beaker.
4. Melt the wax.
5. Pour the wax into a pouring jug (pitcher).
6. Mix the essential oils into the wax.
7. Pour the wax mixture into the mould or container.
8. Allow the candle to set and harden for 24 hours.

Each recipe has its own set of instructions, so follow these accordingly and refer back to these pages for anything you are unsure of.

TROUBLE-SHOOTING

The most common problems encountered when making candles are linked to the size and type of wick, or pouring the wax at too hot a temperature. The best thing is to make a few candles for yourself first and once you are happy with what you have created and have made the mistakes, then you can go on to make impressive gifts for friends and relatives. In other words, a Christmas present production line of candles is not to be recommended without prior home testing! You will find below various issues you may come across when making candles with advice on how to avoid them.

Craters/cracks on the candle

Wax shrinks as it cools and this sometimes creates cracks and craters. When making tapers or pillars in moulds, you can solve this by 'topping off' the wax by adding a little more to fill the hole. To do this, reheat the wax and carefully pour a small amount of wax into the top of the mould. This can happen at the bottom of the candle, but because it is less visible there it doesn't usually present a problem.

You may be experiencing cracks on the sides or tops of your candle, however – cracks on the top of container candles, especially, can be very frustrating. This usually means that you are pouring the wax too hot, so wait for it to cool a little more and ensure that the room is at a constant temperature when you are working.

If you are using a large container, it can be wise to do a two-stage pour. So fill your container about three-quarters full and, once it starts to look like cream cheese (meaning that it is still soft), then do your final pour. If you use this technique and find you are getting a line between the two stages of pouring, then you may be leaving it a little too late for the second pour. This can also be avoided by using a coloured or frosted container or tin.

There are also various types of wax and there is an element of trial and error to establish which wax suits the wicks you are using and which type suits essential oils, as opposed to fragrance oils.

Air bubbles

This can be a problem when using a two-stage pour if you leave it too long in between pours. Air bubbles can also occur if you stir the wax too vigorously when mixing in the essential oils. So have a safety pin at the ready to pop any bubbles that look like they may set.

The candle cores down the middle

Coring is usually due to the wick being too small for the size of the container, so if this happens try a larger size wick. When burning a candle, sufficient time needs to be given for the wax to melt across the top of the container, so if after an hour of burning this has not been achieved then it will almost certainly be because the wick is too small. Remember, too, that if a candle is extinguished before it has time to melt across the top, you are in danger of starting a coring effect.

The wax is not sticking uniformly to a glass container

This is called a 'wet spot' and occurs where the wax has not adhered directly to the glass. You can try warming the glass a little before pouring the wax (just heat it lightly with a hairdryer), but this does sometimes happen for no apparent reason. It does not affect the burning of the candle, so is not a cause for concern.

The candle flame flickers

This is almost certainly a result of having a wick that is too large for the candle – the flame is burning up too much wax and therefore running out of fuel.

The flame is very small and/or spluttering

This will most likely be because the wick is too small and is drowning in the wax pool, so try a larger wick.

The candle is smoking

If you have a smoking candle, make sure the candle is not in a draft. Also, check the wick size, because if it is too large or too long it may smoke. The wick should be a length of about 0.5cm. Always trim the wick before lighting a candle.

The candle taper drips down one side

A dripping taper is caused by the wick not being central in the candle. It can also be a result of the wick not being large enough, or simply being the wrong style of wick.

The candle doesn't smell enough

If you have been working with a certain essential oil, you may find your sense of smell diminishes in connection to that particular oil for a bit. Solutions to refresh your sense of smell are to smell some fresh coffee beans or go outside for a blast of fresh air. Also, you may need to burn more than one candle, especially if you have a large room.

Another reason for a lack of perfume could be that the wax was too hot when you added your oils to the melted wax, in which case the essential oils will evaporate. Indeed, some essential oils have a higher evaporation rate than others, so make sure that you have blended the oils separately so that they 'fix' together.

It is also possible that the essential oil you have is a dilute version, which means the aroma has been thinned and will not smell as strongly. You could then try adding more oils to your blend, but don't exceed a proportion of 7% essential oils to the amount of wax.

The candle has marks and/or a powdery surface

Some fragrance oils/essential oils can cause marks – usually this is the wax cooling down too quickly or the oils not having been blended sufficiently. Avoid this by keeping the room at a consistent, warm temperature. Candles also sometimes react with a mould release spray – this can be solved by placing the candle in the freezer for half an hour. The candle burns down too quickly. This can be caused by the wick being too big or, in the case of tapers using the wrong wick. For tapers, always use a square braided style of wick.

USING ESSENTIAL OILS IN CANDLES

As a quick reference the main properties of some of the more commonly used essential oils are listed here. Their aromas, astrological correspondence and the psychological and magical effects associated with the oils are all included.

While essential oils are a natural product, it is important to remember that they are still chemicals, and strong ones at that. Always take note of any warnings on the labels and take care when handling the oils. I recommend that you wear surgical gloves, or at the very least, make sure you wash your hands immediately if your skin comes into direct contact with them. Some people may have skin sensitivity issues and sensitivity can build up over time.

Essential oils are expensive, so shop around for suppliers. Those offering a wide selection of bottle sizes, for example 10 ml (2 tsp) to 100 ml+ (3½ fl oz+), are usually the most price competitive for the crafter. When you start buying oils it is a good idea to build up your collection slowly, familiarizing yourself with the different price points, smells and the effects different oils have when blended. It is wise to buy from a reputable supplier in order to be sure of the purity of the oils. If you buy something that has been diluted, that is fine, provided you are aware that is the case and that it is compatible with wax, for example, rose and jasmine essential oils are often available diluted in grapeseed oil due to the expense of the absolute.

In the perfume industry, attention has to be given to the evaporation rates of the oil as well as the 'notes' that individual oils have, described as 'top', 'middle' and 'base', referring to the depth of fragrance. While still relevant, this is not quite so imperative with candle-making, as the wax helps to hold in the oils, making it easier to create depth in an aroma. Blending aromas according to their psychological and magical properties also creates a different emphasis and focus for the candle-maker. For example, mint and basil are herbs associated with prosperity in folklore and when blended together they create a wonderful fresh, invigorating and stimulating aroma – sharpening mental capacity can only be a good thing where money matters are concerned. The perfume is said to be beneficial, helping to create a clear and stimulated mind! It can be delightful how wonderful (and somehow appropriate) aromas are when concocting them with a purpose or season in mind, as opposed to just creating a great smell.

COMMONLY USED ESSENTIAL OILS

Basil
Aromatic qualities: green, warming, mildly sweet
Ruler: Mars
Psychological associations: strength and clarity of mind, harmonizing
Magical influences: attracting money, business, harmony and friends

Bay
Aromatic qualities: herbaceous with a spicy edge
Ruler: Sun
Psychological associations: stimulating and energizing
Magical influences: prophecies, visions, protection. Can be combined with other oils for banishing and hexing.

Benzoin
Aromatic qualities: warming, round and vanilla-like
Ruler: Venus
Psychological: comforting, creates a sense of well-being
Magical influences: lends power to other herbs, conscious mind

Bergamot
Aromatic qualities: smoky floral tones, Earl Grey tea
Ruler: Sun
Psychological associations: refreshing and uplifting
Magical influences: happiness, restful sleep

Black pepper
Aromatic qualities: spicy yet cooling
Ruler: Mars
Psychological: motivating, penetrating
Magical influences: courage, mental alertness

Camphor
Aromatic qualities: sharp, pungent, cooling
Ruler: Moon
Psychological: calming and clearing
Magical influences: cleansing, banishing, celibacy,
   healing

Cardamon
Aromatic qualities: sweet, spicy and warming
Ruler: Mars
Psychological: captivating, uplifting
Magical influences: love in compelling and
   commanding way, a catalyst when combined with
   other oils

Cedar
Aromatic qualities: woody, spicy, balsamic and
   camphorous undertone
Ruler: Sun
Psychological associations: soothing and regenerative
Magical influences: psychic work in a protective manner

Camomile
Aromatic qualities: floral with green notes, warming
Ruler: Moon
Psychological: calming, relaxing, soporific
Magical influences: an attracting herb in money and
   luck. Calming, sleep inducing, curse removing.

Cinnamon
Aromatic qualities: warm, spicy woody
Ruler: Sun
Psychological: energizing, restorative, invigorating
Magical influences: love in a lustful way, money, healing,
   a catalyst in baneful sorcery

Citronella
Aromatic qualities: citrus, sharp but with a green note
Ruler: Moon
Psychological: refreshing, invigorating
Magical influences: attracting oil used for friendships
   and business

Citus (Labdanum)
Aromatic qualities: dry, sweet herbaceous, warm, musky
Ruler: Sun
Psychological: sedating, meditative
Magical influences: solar rituals, meditation, general
   well-being

Clary sage
Aromatic qualities: green floral, warm, slight musky
   undertone
Ruler: Moon
Psychological: calming, can be euphoric in large
   amounts
Magical influences: dream work, emotional healing

Clove
Aromatic qualities: warm, woody spicy slightly fruity
   overtone
Ruler: Jupiter
Psychological: warming and soothing
Magical influences: commanding catalyst adding power
   and strength

Cyprus
Aromatic qualities: green fresh woody, slightly balsamic
Ruler: Saturn
Psychological: restorative, emotionally soothing
Magical influences: contact with those that have
   passed, healing

Fennel

Aromatic qualities: aniseed, sweetly herbaceous

Ruler: Mercury

Psychological: resolve, strengthening, stimulating

Magical influences: to effect change, chaos, hex removal

Frankincense

Aromatic qualities: lemony woody, spicy

Ruler: Sun

Psychological: rejuvenating, uplifting, used for inner peace and calm

Magical influences: meditation, heighten awareness of spiritual vibrations, prosperity, balance when combined with Myrrh

Geranium

Aromatic qualities: deeply floral, heady, green tone

Ruler: Venus

Psychological: balancing, focusing

Magical influences: love, protection, well-being

Ginger

Aromatic qualities: spicy oriental, earthy

Ruler: Mars

Psychological: warming, stimulating, aphrodisiac

Magical influences: passion, fire, desire, great energy catalyst

Grapefruit

Aromatic qualities: citrus lemony with woody undertone

Ruler: Jupiter

Psychological: stimulating, refreshing, restoring

Magical influences: healing, protection

Honeysuckle

Aromatic qualities: floral, sweet, fresh

Ruler: Jupiter

Psychological: warming, well-being, musing

Magical influences: prosperity, heightening awareness of psychic realms

Hyssop

Aromatic qualities: floral, sweetly deep and heady

Ruler: Jupiter

Psychological: clarifying, anxiety alleviating, brightening

Magical influences: consecrating, purification, protection

Jasmine

Aromatic qualities: exotic floral, lightly heady

Ruler: Venus

Psychological: desire, aphrodisiac, sensual, harmonizing, innovating,

Magical influences: seduction, dream work

Lavender

Aromatic qualities: herbaceous green floral, high altitude is less herbaceous

Ruler: Mercury

Psychological: calming, relaxing

Magical influences: cleansing, protecting, love

Lemon

Aromatic qualities: citrus, zingy, cooling, fresh

Ruler: Moon

Psychological: refreshing, concentration

Magical influences: physical energy, healing, purification

Lemongrass

Aromatic qualities: fresh, citrus, zingy, green notes

Ruler: Mercury

Psychological: revitalizing, rejuvenating, euphoric, energizing

Magical influences: positively for increasing psychic power, study of all things magical, negatively to complicate and confuse, the fae (fairies)

Lemon Balm

Aromatic qualities: floral citrus, sharply fresh

Ruler: Jupiter

Psychological: tension reliever, calming, uplifting

Magical influences: cleansing, expanding

Lemon Verbena

Aromatic qualities: floral citrus, fresh
Ruler: Mercury
Psychological: clearing, uplifting
Magical influences: to attract love, luck and general positivity

Mandarin

Aromatic qualities: citrus floral, sweet
Ruler: Mandarin
Psychological: soothing, calming, good for irritable children, harmonizing
Magical influences: luck, love, happiness

Marigold/*Tagetes*

Aromatic qualities: warm, floral earthy
Ruler: Sun
Psychological: happiness, calm, well-being
Magical influence: solar work, legal matter, dreams, power

Myrrh

Aromatic qualities: dry, resinous, slightly musky
Ruler: Moon
Psychological: healing, rejuvenating, soothing
Magical influences: balance when combined with frankincense, healing, meditation, spirituality

Neroli

Aromatic qualities: fresh, delicate, sweet floral
Ruler: Sun
Psychological: reassuring, rejuvenating, euphoric, relaxing
Magical influences: attracting in love matters

Nutmeg

Aromatic qualities: spicy with a hint of the floral
Ruler: Jupiter
Psychological: warming, revitalizing the senses
Magical influences: money, energy, luck

Oakmoss

Aromatic qualities: woody, grassy, mossy
Ruler: Jupiter
Psychological: grounding
Magical influences: money, power

Orange

Aromatic qualities: sweet citrus
Ruler: Sun
Psychological: detoxifying, creates happiness and well-being, soothing
Magical influences: magical energy, joy

Palmarose

Aromatic qualities: sweet, floral, green
Ruler: Venus
Psychological: relieving, strengthening, soothing
Magical influences: to strengthen other love and healing oils

Patchouli

Aromatic qualities: heady, earthy, spicy woody, warming
Ruler: Saturn
Psychological: grounding, sensual, diminishes conscious thought
Magical influences: lust, power, money, manifesting desires

Peppermint

Aromatic qualities: freshly herbaceous
Ruler: Mercury
Psychological: cooling, stimulates the mind, focusing, refreshing
Magical influences: mints in general terms are purifying and associated with money matters

Petitgrain

Aromatic qualities: citrus green, leafy, zingy
Ruler: Sun
Psychological: energizing, invigorating, rejuvenating, liberating
Magical influences: protection

Pine
Aromatic qualities: fresh, woody, resinous
Ruler: Saturn
Psychological: cleansing, refreshing, opening
Magical influences: healing, uncrossing, grounding

Rose
Aromatic qualities: soft, floral, slight lemony undertone
Ruler: Venus
Psychological: nurturing, restoring, strengthening, sensual
Magical influences: love, peace, beauty

Rosemary
Aromatic qualities: herbaceous, slightly camphorous, woody balsamic
Ruler: Sun
Psychological: focuses the mind, clearing, stimulating
Magical influences: protection, purification, mental alertness, longevity, ancestors

Sage
Aromatic qualities: herbaceous, woody
Ruler: Jupiter
Psychological: stimulating, clearing
Magical influences: protection, longevity, purification

Sandalwood
Aromatic qualities: resinous woody, lightly heady
Ruler: Moon
Psychological: sensual, harmonizing, unifying
Magical influences: sensuality, heighten spiritual vibrations, clairvoyance

Sweet Marjoram
Aromatic qualities: herbaceous, camphorous, sweet undertone
Ruler: Mercury
Psychological: soothing, clearing
Magical influences: peace, celibacy, sleep, healing

Teatree
Aromatic qualities: fresh, green herbaceous, antiseptic
Ruler: Mercury
Psychological: stimulating, invigorating
Magical influences: healing, conscious mental activity

Thyme
Aromatic qualities: herbaceous, camphorous, oriental undertone
Ruler: Venus
Psychological: clearing, uplifting
Magical influences: spirits, positive vibrations, cleansing, courage, psychic powers

Vanilla
Aromatic qualities: warm, exotic, sultry
Ruler: Venus
Psychological: sensual, affection, warmth, revitalizing
Magical influences: seduction, lust, love, magical energy

Vetivert
Aromatic qualities: heady, smoky earthy
Ruler: Saturn
Psychological: nourishing, grounding, restorative
Magical influences: uncrossing, protecting, money

Ylang Ylang
Aromatic qualities: warm, sensual, exotic round floral
Ruler: Venus
Psychological: sensual, relaxing
Magical influences: attracting love and attention

SAFETY FIRST

The following advice is all common sense. However, please read through carefully as you should never become complacent when working with a heat source in combination with wax and oils. These projects are not suitable for children under the age of 12 and those older than 12 should be supervised by an adult at all times.

- Always allow wax pellets to melt slowly using a low heat (ie. not on a heat).
- When melting your wax always use a double boiler.
- Never, ever, leave your wax on a heat source unattended because if it overheats it will catch fire.
- Do not melt wax directly on the heat source and never use a microwave – there is a danger of the wax catching fire. You need to boil your water in the receptacle that forms the base of the double boiler, turn it down to a simmer and then add your jug, can or top saucepan.
- Always allow your wax pellets to melt slowly on a low heat.
- If the wax starts to bubble, it is too hot.
- If you are using a thermometer, follow the manufacturer's instructions regarding melt point, desirable pouring point and set point.
- Place your jug with the melted wax on an old chopping board if it is hot so that you don't mark work surfaces or melt work mats.
- If using tin cans, remember that the rim may be sharp.
- When mixing and using essential oils, use a mat or chopping board to work on – some essential oils can mark work surfaces.
- Always use a dish towel or oven gloves (mitts) to remove your jug, saucepan or can from the double boiler – it will be hot. This is another reason to turn off the heat source when removing your jug: if the edges of the dish towel or oven gloves catch the heat source by accident, you may start a fire.
- Turn off the heat source before removing the wax from the double boiler in case you accidently drip any wax.
- Source candle containers from a specialist candle supplier so that they are fit for purpose.
- Should you accidently get essential oils on your skin and develop a severe reaction, seek advice from your medical practitioner immediately.

CONVERSION CHART FOR ESSENTIAL OILS

As an approximate guide, 20 drops of essential oils equal 1 millilitre. This will depend on the viscosity of the oil and the size of drop, but this is a safe guide. This guide is used in the conversion chart below, so test the number of drops your dropper creates for 1ml water first and, if you need to, change the conversion amounts accordingly.

0.5 ml		10 drops
1 ml		20 drops
1.5 ml	¼ tsp	30 drops
2 ml		40 drops
2.5 ml	½ tsp	50 drops
3 ml		60 drops
3.5 ml		70 drops
3.75 ml	¾ tsp	75 drops
4 ml		80 drops
4.5 ml		90 drops
5 ml	1 tsp	100 drops
7.5 ml	1½ tsp	150 drops
8 ml		160 drops
10 ml	2 tsp	200 drops
11 ml		220 drops
12.5 ml	2 ½ tsp	250 drops
15 ml	3 tsp	300 drops
17.5 ml	3½ tsp	350 drops
20 ml	4 tsp	400 drops
25 ml	1½ tbsp	500 drops
30 ml	2 tbsp	600 drops

Making A Rolled Beeswax Taper

These natural tapers can be made delightfully quickly and are available in all sorts of colours, so are excellent for themed occasions. Children love to roll the candles, and so, providing any cutting of the sheets is undertaken by an adult, they can make great holiday projects!

YOU WILL NEED

- beeswax sheet
- square braided wick
- sharp knife
- cutting ruler
- cutting board

METHOD

1. Cut the beeswax sheet in half at an angle, to give the top of the candle a tapered appearance. This technique is all about the look of the candle and it does make the burn time quite short, so you can always use the whole sheet instead of cutting it, if you like.

NOTE

If the sheet is too cold it will become brittle and crack, so it is important to work in a warm atmosphere. If you taper the top, then it is crucial to use a sharp knife and a safety ruler (these are triangular in shape and available at most craft stores) – this stops the knife from running over the edge of the ruler and giving you a nasty cut.

2. Cut the wick to size, leaving about 1 cm (½ in) at the top.

3. Carefully place the wick flat on the edge of the beeswax and start to roll the beeswax around the wick.

4. Then slowly roll the rest of the sheet.

Making A Hand-Dipped Taper

Making your own dipped beeswax tapers is incredibly satisfying – nothing quite beats the natural honey-like aroma, and the more you make the better the tapers become.

YOU WILL NEED

- 1.5 kg (3 lb 5 oz) beeswax pellets,or enough to fill the capacity of your dipping container
- cotton square braided wick
- dipping and melting vat boiler
- dip gripper or oven gloves (mitts)
- candle dye (optional)
- essential oils (optional)

NOTES

As you work, you will probably need to top up the level of beeswax, in which case return the pan and vat to the hob, add more beeswax and melt it before continuing.

When making coloured or fragrance beeswax tapers, it is advisable to use two dipping vats, one for dipping the wicks to make the tapers and another for melting wax for 'topping up' the dipping vat. If you don't do this, it will be difficult to get the colour or the essential oils consistent.

METHOD

1. Cover the floor with newspaper or a vinyl sheet. suspend a 5 cm (2 in) wide piece of wood between two chairs and stand them on the newspaper or vinyl.

2. Half fill the dipping vat with hot water. Bring to a boil, then turn the heat down to a simmer.

3. Fill the melting vat with beeswax pellets and place the vat in the pan. Allow the beeswax to melt, then top the vat up with more pellets until the level of the liquid wax is a few centimetres (an inch or so) from the top. If you are adding dye, do so at this point and mix everything thoroughly. Test the colour by dripping a tiny bit of wax onto a piece of paper – the wax in the vat will appear darker than it is in reality.

4. The pan handles may be hot, so using oven gloves (mitts), remove the pan from the hob and place it on a wooden chopping board on the floor. Now add any essential oils, if required. (SAFETY NOTE: Do not dip the candles while the pan is on the hob or heat source because you would be exposing dripped wax to naked flames or a direct heat source which could cause a fire.)

5. Dip both ends of the wick into the vat, one at a time. Some people like to add a metal nut to the bottom of the wick to help keep it straight

6. On the first dip you will need to gently straighten the wick after dipping, then hang up the taper to dry. Do the same to all the wicks), then go back to the first one and dip it in the wax again. Keep this process going until the taper has reached your desired width (it takes around 25–35 dips for a taper). If candle dipping is something that you are going to be doing regularly, it may be worth investing in a dipping tool to enable you to do more than one at a time and to help keep the

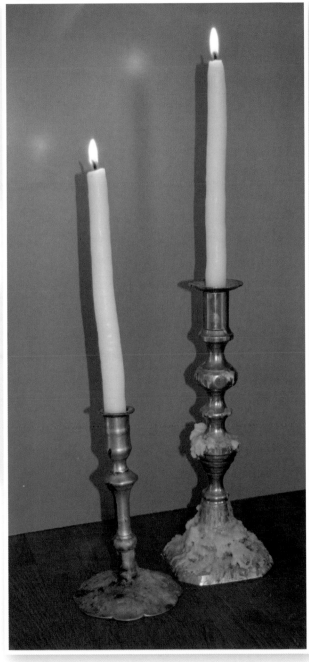

Candles for Mood and Wellbeing

Positivity

Enjoy beautiful fresh, clear aromas in a neat little glass container. The oils combine in this candle to create an atmosphere of positivity and clarity – think herbaceous and balsamic, with a mild, marginally sweet, spicy undertone.

YOU WILL NEED

- 125 ml (4½ fl oz) glass pot, 50 cm (h) x 70 cm (d) (20 x 27½ in)
- 125 g (4½ oz) container soy wax
- wick, sustainer and wax glue
- splints and elastic band
- 5 ml (100 drops) rosemary essential oil
- 3 ml (60 drops) bay essential oil
- 1 ml (20 drops) myrrh essential oil
- 2 ml (40 drops) basil essential oil
- double boiler
- pipettes, for the essential oils
- small container or beaker
- pouring jug (pitcher)

METHOD

1. Measure the wick against the height of the container, leaving an extra 4 cm (1½ in) for a knot and the splint wick supports. Knot the wick at the base and thread it through the sustainer. Place a blob of wax glue on the base of the sustainer and stick this in the centre of the glass pot base.

2. Weigh the wax and melt it in the double boiler.

3. While the wax is melting, mix together the essential oils in a small container.

4. When the wax has melted, pour 125 ml (4½ fl oz) wax into the pouring jug (pitcher) and allow it to cool for a few minutes.

5. Add the essential oil mixture to the melted wax and stir thoroughly to ensure an even distribution of the oils in the wax.

6. Pour the mixture into the glass container and allow it to set for 24 hours. Trim the wick prior to use.

Uplifting

This stimulating, zingy candle incorporates a selection of oils that are associated with uplifting the mood, psychic development and divination.

YOU WILL NEED

- pillar candle mould, 300 ml (½ pint) capacity
- 320 g (11½ oz) beeswax
- silicon mould release spray
- square braided wick
- splints and elastic bands
- candle dye (optional)
- 11 ml (220 drops) lemongrass essential oil
- 1 ml (20 drops) bay essential oil
- 3 ml (60 drops) thyme essential oil
- double boiler
- pipettes, for the essential oils
- small container or beaker
- pouring jug (pitcher)
- Tupperware or old ice cream container, to hold candle mould

METHOD

1. Spray the mould with a silicon mould release. Thread the wick through the hole in the base of the mould and seal in place with modelling putty. Leave about 7 cm (2¾ in) of wick at the top of the mould (this will be the candle base) to give you something to hold on to when pulling the candle out of the mould.

2. Using a splint, make sure the wick is central to the mould and that it is straight and taut.

3. Weigh 320 g (11½ oz) wax and melt it in the double boiler. If you are using candle dye, then add it now.

4. Mix the essential oils together in a small container. When the wax is fully melted, pour 300ml (½ pint) beeswax into the pouring jug (pitcher), then mix in the essential oils until fully blended.

5. Place the mould in a plastic container.

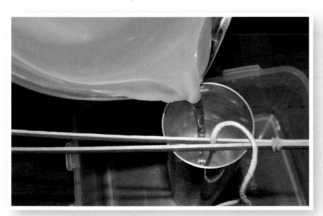

6. Pour the blended wax into the mould. Check that the wick is still central. Once it has set but is still warm to the touch, you will probably notice that the wax has pulled away from the wick leaving a hole. Melt a little leftover wax and pour it into the hole.

7. Leave for 24 hours before pulling the candle out of the mould. If this proves difficult, put the mould into the freezer for an hour and try again.

Health

Essential oils of Clary Sage, Rosemary,
Marjoram & Lavender for aromas associated with
good health, well being, healing and calm.
A natural soy wax candle handcrafted in West Sussex.

The Hedgewitches' Garden

Love

candle melts with essential oils of
...marose, Orange el dried Rose Petals
...poured in West Sussex.

Hedgewitches' Garden

Kitchen Witch

...banish unwanted cooking and kitchen smells. A hand
...de in West Sussex with essential oils of Lemongrass,
...all associated with purification and uplifting.

Hedgewitches' Garden

Energizing

This faceted glass candle helps to create a magical, sparkly light, which is magnified by its many sides. The aromas are woody, balsamic, spicy and warming. The bay and orange are power oils in this context, the ginger is fiery and imbibes passion and the pine helps you to focus.

YOU WILL NEED

- Facetted 160 ml (5¼ fl oz) glass candleholder
- 160 g (5¼ oz) container soy wax
- wick, sustainers and wax glue
- 2 ml (40 drops) bay essential oil
- 5 ml (100 drops) orange essential oil
- 2 ml (40 drops) ginger essential oil
- 2 ml (40 drops) pine essential oil
- double boiler
- pipettes, for the essential oils
- small container or beaker
- pouring jug (pitcher)

METHOD

1. Measure and cut the wick by taking the height of the container and adding 2 cm (¾ in), then tie a knot at one end and push the other end through the sustainer. Secure on the base of the glass with a blob of wax glue. Position with the splints and elastic bands, making sure that the wick is straight and taut.

2. Weigh 160g (5¼ fl oz) wax and melt it in the double boiler.

3. Blend the essential oils together in a small container. When the wax is fully melted, pour 160 ml (5¼ fl oz) into the pouring jug, leave to stand for a couple of minutes before adding the essential oils, mixing them thoroughly into the wax.

4. Pour the blended wax into the glass. As this is a large container, it is important to work in a warm atmosphere to allow the wax to cool slowly and minimize the chance of the wax cracking on the surface.

5. Leave to set for 24 hours, then remove the splints and trim the wick.

Amour

Enjoy these beautiful rich red beeswax tapers, which have been scented for love with floral aromas and sweet citrus overtones. The moulds produce tapers measuring 23.5 x 2.2cm (9¼ x ¾ in) with a burn time of around 6 hours (this would increase to about 8 hours without the dye and essential oils).

YOU WILL NEED

- taper moulds
- 600 g (1 lb 6 oz) beeswax
- silicon mould release spray
- modelling putty
- splints and elastic bands
- deep red candle dye
- 2 ml (40 drops) rose essential oil
- 6 ml (120 drops) geranium essential oil
- 9 ml (180 drops) palmarose essential oil
- 21 ml (420 drops) orange essential oil
- double boiler
- pipettes, for the essential oils
- small container or beaker
- pouring jug (pitcher)

METHOD

1. Spray the mould with the mould release spray. Work out how much wax the moulds are going to take. Melt the beeswax in the double boiler.

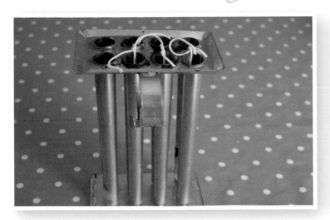

2. Meanwhile, thread the wick through the mould (patience is required at this point if you are using an antique-style tin mould).

3. To seal the mould, place some reusable putty on the base where the top of the candle will eventually be – this stops the wax from leaking. Make sure the wicks are taut, straight and down the centre of each chamber. Secure the wicks with the splints.

4. When the beeswax has melted, add the candle dye. Test the dye by putting a couple of drips of wax on some paper until the desired depth of colour is obtained. Remove the wax from the double boiler and pour the required amount of wax, 600ml (1 pint) in this case, into the pouring jug (pitcher).

5. Mix the essential oils together, stir into the beeswax and pour carefully into the taper mould chambers. Leave for about 1 hour to set and check to see whether you have wax pull holes. Top these up with any leftover wax and leave for 24 hours before pulling the tapers out of the mould. If this proves difficult, put the mould into the freezer for an hour and try again.

Happiness

The aromas in this candle are all about directing your energy to make you feel good about yourself. The sweet, warming citrus overtones with a hint of the floral and a slightly musky undertone will create an atmosphere of warmth and pleasure.

YOU WILL NEED

- 85 ml (3 fl oz) capacity glass votive candle holder
- 85 g (3½ oz) container soy wax
- wick, sustainers and wax glue
- splints and elastic bands
- 3 ml (60 drops) orange essential oil
- 1 ml (20 drops) marigold (tagettes) essential oil
- 0.5 ml (10 drops) bergamot essential oil
- 0.5 ml (10 drops) rosemary essential oil
- double boiler
- pipettes, for the essential oils
- small container or beaker
- pouring jug (pitcher)

METHOD

1. Cut the wick to size and knot one end. Fix it to the centre of the glass votive base using wax glue and secure with a couple of splints.

2. Weigh 85g (3½ oz) wax and melt in the double boiler. Because this candle uses just a small amount of wax you might like to use the tin can method (see page 9).

3. Blend the essential oils together in a small container. When the wax is fully melted, pour 80ml (5 tbsp) into the pouring jug (pitcher). Leave to stand for a couple of minutes before adding the essential oils.

4. Pour the blended wax into the glass votive and leave it to cool for 24 hours before trimming the wick.

Sensual

These aromas are warming, sweet and floral with heady, spicy undertones. The vanilla and jasmine are warming and relaxing, ylang ylang is sensual, the patchouli adds a heady, compelling power to the aroma and the sandalwood a sense of ritual.

YOU WILL NEED

- a small glass pot around approximately, 5 cm (h) x 7 cm (d) (2 x 3 in), capacity 100 ml (3½ fl oz)
- 100 g (3½ oz) soy wax
- wick, sustainer and wax glue
- splints and elastic bands
- 2 ml (40 drops) vanilla fragrance oil
- 1 ml (20 drops) jasmine essential oil
- 1 ml (20 drops) ylang ylang essential oil
- 1 ml (20 drops) ginger essential oil
- 1 ml (20 drops) sandalwood essential oils
- pipettes, for the essential oils
- small container or beaker

METHOD

1. Measure the wick against the height of the container leaving an extra 4cm (1½ in) for a knot and the splint wick supports. Knot the wick at the base and thread it through the sustainer. Place a blob of wax glue on the base of the sustainer and stick it in the centre of the base of the glass pot with a little wax glue.

2. Weigh the soy wax and melt it in the double boiler.

3. While the wax is melting, mix together the essential oils in a small container.

4. When the wax has melted, pour it into the pouring jug (pitcher) and allow it to cool slightly. Add the essential oil mixture to the melted wax and stir thoroughly to ensure the even distribution of the oils throughout the wax.

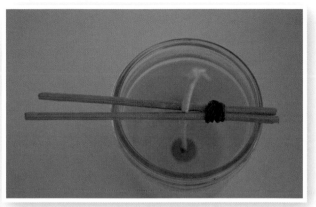

5. Pour the mixture into the glass container and allow it to set for 24 hours. Trim the wick prior to use and finish off the look with a gold-coloured lid.

Refreshing

This candle will create zingy, herbaceous, uplifting aromas that will cut through any unwanted cooking smells, freshen up a room or simply allow you to enjoy the sweet smell of lemongrass.

YOU WILL NEED

- container with 250 ml (8 fl oz) capacity
- 250 g (9 oz) container soy wax
- wick, sustainer and wax glue
- splints and elastic bands
- 10 ml (200 drops) lemongrass essential oil
- 5 ml (100 drops) rosemary essential oil
- double boiler
- pipettes, for the essential oils
- small container or beaker
- pouring jug (pitcher)

METHOD

1. Knot the wick and thread it through the sustainer. Fix the wick to the base of the container with wax glue and use splints to keep the wick straight, taut and central. Place the tin on a heatproof surface, such as a wooden chopping board.

2. Weigh 250 g (9 oz) wax and melt it in the double boiler.

3. Blend the essential oils together in a small container.

4. Pour 250 ml (8 fl oz) melted wax into the pouring jug (pitcher), allow it to stand for a few minutes, then mix in the essential oils. .

5. Pour into the candle container. Leave to cool.

6. Trim the wick.

Concentration

Soy wax melts are an effective way of using essential oils in an oil burner to infuse or change an atmosphere. This refreshing blend of citrus, minty and woody aromas is useful for times when concentration is needed and can also be used for clearing the air if you are feeling overwhelmed and confused.

YOU WILL NEED

- 4 small moulds, each containing around 25ml (1 ½ tbsp) of wax
- 85 g (3 oz) pillar soy wax
- 20 g (¾ oz) pillar rapeseed wax
- 1.5 ml (30 drops) rosemary essential oil
- 1 ml (20 drops) mint essential oil
- 1 ml (20 drops) cypress essential oil
- 2.5 ml (50 drops) lemon essential oil
- a couple of strips dried lemon peel, chopped, or a sprinkle of dried rosemary
- double boiler
- pipettes, for the essential oils
- small container or beaker
- pouring jug (pitcher)

HOW TO USE MELTS

Place the candle melt in the bowl) of your oil burner – there is no need to add water. Light an unscented tealight in the base of the oil burner. The candle melt will gradually turn to liquid wax and slowly release the essential oil aromas. If you extinguish the tealight, the wax will set and be ready to use again. Keep using the melt until there are no aromas coming from the wax. Remove the unscented wax by refrigerating for 15 minutes; this will make the wax shrink away from the sides of the bowl so that you can remove it.

METHOD

1. Sprinkle the dried ingredients into each mould. Blend the essential oils together in a small container.

2. Weigh the soy and rapeseed waxes and melt them in the double boiler, making sure you have enough for 4 moulds.

3. Pour the 100ml (3¾ fl oz) wax into the pouring jug (pitcher) and mix in the essential oils.

4. Pour the wax into the melt moulds and leave them to set.

5. Once the melts are set, turn the wax out of the moulds. If you have any difficulty, leave them in the refrigerator for about 15 minutes. Store the melts in an airtight container or sealed plastic bag. Leave for 24 hours before using.

Harmony

Create a harmonious atmosphere with this herbaceous, citrus melt. Basil promotes sympathy and is good for soothing the nerves, lemon signifies friendship and bergamot is associated with clarity and putting things in good working order.

YOU WILL NEED

- Tupperware container, 15 x 22 x 8 cm (16 x 9 x 3 in)
- 175 g (6 oz) pillar soy wax
- 30 g (1 oz) pillar rapeseed wax
- 3 ml (60 drops) basil essential oil
- 7 ml (140 drops) lemon essential oil
- 2 ml (40 drops) bergamot essential oil
- double boiler
- pipettes, for the essential oils
- small container or beaker
- pouring jug (pitcher)

METHOD

1. Blend the essential oils together in a small container.

2. Weigh the soy and pillar waxes and put them into the double boiler. Once the wax has melted, pour it into the pouring jug (pitcher) and mix in the essential oils.

3. Pour the blended wax into the Tupperware container and allow it to set for 24 hours.

4. Refrigerate the container for about 20 minutes.

5. Break the wax into shards and store the pieces in a glass jar so you can remove them as you need them.

Meditation

This aromatic blend uses oils with ritual associations which have a transdescent quality, with deep, woody notes and balsamic undertones. These oils are expensive but do produce wonderful aromas.

YOU WILL NEED

- 4 small moulds, each containing around 25 ml (1½ tbsp) wax
- 85 g (3 oz) pillar soy wax
- 20 g (¾ oz) pillar rapeseed wax
- 3 ml (60 drops) sandalwood essential oil
- 3 ml (60 drops) frankincense essential oil
- double boiler
- pipettes, for the essential oils
- small container or beaker
- pouring jug (pitcher)

METHOD

1. Sprinkle the dried ingredients into each mould.

2. Blend the essential oils together in a small container.

3. Weigh the soy and rapeseed waxes and melt them in the double boiler, making sure you have enough for 4 moulds.

4. Pour the wax into the pouring jug (pitcher) and mix in the essential oils.

5. Pour the wax into the moulds and leave to set.

6. Turn the set wax out of the moulds. If you have any difficulty, Irefrigerate them for about 15 minutes. Store the melts in an airtight container or sealed plastic bag. Leave for 24 hours before using.

NOTES

You can, of course, add all sorts of colours to candle melts and be creative with the herbs that you include, for example, dried lavender will help increase the aromatic quality of the melt. There are also all sorts of candle melt moulds available – just be sure that the one you choose is the right size for your oil burner.

Relaxing

These tealights are floral and herbaceous with warming vanilla undertones. Lighting one after a hard day's work will help to disperse some of the tensions accumulated throughout the day.

YOU WILL NEED

- 10 tealight foil or plastic containers
- 200 g (7oz) container soy wax
- 10 tealight wicks with sustainers
- 8 ml (160 drops) lavender essential oil
- 2 ml (40 drops) clary sage essential oil
- 2 ml (40 drops) benzoin essential oil
- double boiler
- pipettes, for the essential oils
- small container or beaker
- pouring jug (pitcher)

METHOD

1. Mix together the essential oils in a small container.

2. Weigh the wax and place it in the double boiler. Melt the wax.

3. Pour the wax into the wax jug (pitcher) and add the essential oil mixture, stirring thoroughly.

4. Pour the wax mixture into the tealight containers. Leave for a minute and then add the tealight wicks in the centre of the containers.

5. Leave the tealights to set for 24 hours prior to use. The tealight wicks are specially designed for tealights so there is no need to trim them.

Sleep-Inducing

This dreamy blend of essential oils takes the effect of relaxation aromas one stage further, creating an atmosphere with strong, herbaceous top notes and sweet, balsamic undertones that will help induce sleep.

YOU WILL NEED [B]

- 4 wax tart moulds
- 85 g (3 oz) pillar soy wax
- 20 g (¾ oz) pillar rapeseed wax
- 4 ml (80 drops) drops lavender essential oil
- 2 ml (40 drops) camomile essential oil
- dried lavender or camomile, enough to scatter on the base of the moulds
- double boiler
- pipettes, for the essential oils
- small container or beaker
- pouring jug (pitcher)

METHOD

1. Place the dried lavender or camomile into each mould.

2. Blend the essential oils together in the small container.

3. Weigh the soy and rapeseed waxes and melt them together in the double boiler, making sure you have enough for the 4 moulds.

4. Pour all the wax into the pouring jug (pitcher) and mix in the essential oils.

5. Pour the wax into the moulds and leave to set. These plastic moulds keep the melts fresh and you can break off a cube each time you want a new melt.

Bereavement

The oils used in this candle are blended to be thought-provoking, calming and connected with respect and memory. The idea is that the candle is lit for an hour each day to help heal the pain of loss. Alternatively, it can be used as an annual advent to celebrate an individual's life. Using a lidded glass jar for the mould creates a candle with a lid, which signifies closure when not in use. This is ideal as a gift in times of sorrow. Some people like to add the name or an image and maybe some dates so that it becomes more personalised.

YOU WILL NEED

- 250 ml (8 fl oz) glass jar
- 250 g (9 oz) container soy wax
- wick, sustainers and wax glue
- splints and elastic bands
- 4 ml (80 drops) lavender essential oil
- 3 ml (60 drops) tansy essential oil
- 1 ml (20 drops) marjoram essential oil
- 4 ml (80 drops) rosemary essential oil
- 3 ml (60 drops) clary sage
- double boiler
- pipettes, for the essential oils
- small container or beaker
- pouring jug (pitcher)

METHOD

1. Cut the wick to size and knot it at one end. Thread this through the sustainer and stick it to the centre of the glass base using wax glue. Secure it to the rim with a couple of splints.

2. Weigh and melt the wax in the double boiler.

3. Blend the essential oils together in a small container

4. Pour the melted wax into the pouring jug (pitcher). Leave it to stand for a couple of minutes before adding the essential oils.

5. Pour the blended wax into the glass and leave to cool for 24 hours before trimming the wick.

Celebrate the Season

Meadow

This candle is surprisingly bright as the light reflects off the side of the cup. It makes a wonderful present, particularly if you have been to a pottery studio to paint your own design. The aromas in this recipe are herbaceous, warm and lightly floral and are designed to be relaxing and harmonious.

YOU WILL NEED [B]

- coffee mug with at least 160 ml (¼ pint) capacity
- 160 g (5½ oz) container soy wax
- wick, sustainer and wax glue
- splints and elastic bands
- 1 ml (20 drops) camomile essential oil
- 4 ml (80 drops) lavender essential oil
- 2 ml (40 drops) basil essential oil
- 2 ml (40 drops) lemon verbena essential oil
- double boiler
- pipettes, for the essential oils
- small container or beaker
- pouring jug (pitcher)

METHOD

1. Measure and cut the wick, put a knot at one end and thread it through the sustainer. Fix the sustainer to the base of the mug in a central position using wax glue. Secure the wick with splints.

2. Weigh and melt the wax in the double boiler.

3. Blend the essential oils together in a small container.

4. Pour the melted wax into the pouring jug (pitcher). Leave it to stand for a couple of minutes before adding the essential oils.

5. Pour the blended wax into the mug and leave it to set for 24 hours before trimming the wick.

Persephone's Dawn

The combination of lavender and lemon brings herbaceous but zingy notes to this blend, a touch of the floral with the clary sage and a hint of warmth with the honeysuckle.

YOU WILL NEED

- 1 x 50 ml (1¾ fl oz) capacity candle holder, 3.5 cm (h) x 5 cm (w) (1 x 2 in). I've used a small tin
- 50 g (2 oz) container soy wax
- wick, sustainer and wax glue
- splints and elastic bands
- 1.5 ml (30 drops) lavender essential oil
- 13 drops lemon essential oil
- 6 drops clary sage essential oil
- 6 drops honeysuckle or jasmine essential oil
- double boiler
- pipettes, for the essential oils
- small container or beaker
- pouring jug (pitcher)

METHOD

1. Cut approximately 4.5 cm (1¾ in) of wick and knot it at the base. Thread this through the sustainer and stick it to the centre of the base of the container with a little wax glue. Put the splints around the wick to keep it straight and taut.

2. Weigh 50g (2oz) wax and melt it in the double boiler.

3. While the wax is melting, mix together the essential oils in a small container.

4. When the wax has melted, pour 50ml (1¾ fl oz) of wax into the pouring jug (pitcher) and leave it to cool for a few minutes.

6. Pour the mixture into the tin and allow it to set for 24 hours. Trim the wick prior to use.

5. Add the essential oil mixture to the melted wax and stir thoroughly to ensure an even distribution of the oils in the wax.

Mediterranean Summer

Candles in glass jars are supremely practical for *al fresco* entertaining. The fresh, warming aromas of this candle are tinged with the woody balsamic oils of pine and thyme, which are typically released from Mediterranean trees in the heat of the sun.

YOU WILL NEED

- 250 ml (8 fl oz) capacity glass jar
- 250 g (9 oz) container soy wax
- wick, sustainer and wax glue
- splints and elastic bands
- 8 ml (160 drops) pine essential oil
- 2 ml (40 drops) thyme essential oil
- 3 ml (60 drops) rosemary essential oil
- 2 ml (40 drops) *Tagetes* (marigold) essential oil
- double boiler
- pipettes, for the essential oils
- small container or beaker
- pouring jug (pitcher)

METHOD

1. Knot the wick, thread it through the sustainer and stick it to the centre base of the jar with wax glue. Put the splints around the wick to keep it straight and taut.

2. Weigh 250 g (9 oz) of wax and melt it in the double boiler.

 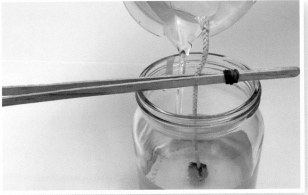

3. Blend the essential oils together in a small container. When the wax has melted, pour 250 ml (8 fl oz) into the pouring jug (pitcher), allow it to stand for a few minutes and then mix in the essential oils.

4. Pour the wax slowly into the jar, making sure that the wick is central. Leave for 24 hours to set.

Mosquito Travel Tin

If you live in an area that is prone to mosquitos, are planning to go travelling, or, like me, seem to be beloved by those annoying buzzy creatures when they ignore the rest of the family, then this one is for you! This candle formula is also a great one to use in candle melts. This blend uses rosemary, lemongrass and citronella, with the first two helping to minimize the sometimes bitter smell of citronella. If you want the citronella to dominate more, you could just use 7 ml (1½ tsp) of citronella oil.

YOU WILL NEED

- 1 x candle container with a 125 ml (4 fl oz) capacity
- 125 g (4¼ oz) container soy wax
- wick, sustainer and wax glue
- splints and elastic bands
- 1.5 ml (30 drops) lemongrass essential oil
- 1.5 ml (30 drops) rosemary essential oil
- 4 ml (80 drops) citronella essential oil
- double boiler
- pipettes, for the essential oils
- small container or beaker
- pouring jug (pitcher)
- [mosquito step 1 materials]

METHOD

1. Knot the wick, thread it through the sustainer and stick it to the base of the tin with wax glue. Put the splints around the wick to keep it straight and taut.

2. Weigh 125 g (4½ oz) of wax and melt it in the double boiler.

3. Blend the essential oils together in a small container. When the wax has melted, pour the wax into the pouring jug (pitcher), allow it to stand few a few minutes and then mix in the essential oils.

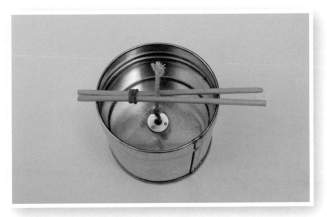

If you are making a few of these candles, leave at least 5 cm (2i n) between each to allow enough air circulation so that the wax cools evenly.

Make sure that the surface you make these candles on is heat resistant – antique furniture and some wooden tabletops can be left with ring marks, so use a terracotta plant saucer or something similar to protect these surfaces.

4. Pour the mixture into the container and allow it to set for 24 hours prior to use. It is important not to pour the wax when it is too hot when using metal containers, because the metal conducts heat extremely well and can make the wax glue dislodge from the base.

Cottage Garden Melts

These wonderful aromatic melts evoke the delights of a cottage garden. The essential oils are sweet and floral, but not sickly due to the balancing fresh, citrus notes of the lemon.

YOU WILL NEED

- 4 small moulds, each containing around 25ml (1½ tbsp) of wax
- 85 g (3 oz) pillar soy wax
- 20 g (¾ oz) pillar rapeseed wax
- dried rose petals, enough to cover the base of the mould
- 1.5 ml (30 drops) geranium essential oil
- 1 ml (20 drops) palmarosa essential oil
- 1 ml (20 drops) basil essential oil
- 2.5 ml (50 drops) lemon essential oil
- double boiler
- pipettes, for the essential oils
- small container or beaker
- pouring jug (pitcher)

METHOD

1. Sprinkle the dried rose petals into each mould.

2. Blend the essential oils together in a small container.

3. Weigh the soy and rapeseed waxes and melt them together in the double boiler.

4. Pour the melted wax into the pouring jug (pitcher) and mix in the essential oils. Pour the wax into the melt moulds and leave them to set.

5. Turn the wax out of the moulds. If you have any difficulty, refrigerate them for about 15 minutes. Leave for 24 hours before using. Store in an airtight container or sealed plastic bag.

Witchy Halloween Tapers

These knobbly, witchy black beeswax tapers are perfect to create a spooky atmosphere, and the scent, a blend of spicy, warming, earthy and heady aromas with a magical quality, is authentic for the witching time of year. This process does takes practice and will create a mess, so make sure that all surfaces and any exposed floor are covered in newspapers or a plastic sheet.

YOU WILL NEED

- 1.2 kg (2½ lb) beeswax black candle dye
- square braided cotton wick
- 10 ml (200 drops) patchouli essential oil
- 30 ml (600 drops) cedarwood essential oil
- 30 ml (600 drops) cinnamon essential oil
- 5 ml (100 drops) cypress essential oil
- pipettes, for the essential oils
- candle-dipping saucepan and containers
- small container or beaker
- a clean, old baking tray, that is no longer used for baking

METHOD

1. Follow the instructions on page 30 for making hand-dipped tapers.

2. Prop up the baking tray at an angle on some books so that the wax will collect at one side. Melt the leftover wax from making the dipped tapers and pour some into the baking tray.

4. When the beeswax starts to solidify, pour in some more wax from the melter. Try to avoid allowing the taper to touch the base of the tray so that it doesn't stick. The more knobbly and strange they look the better! Hang the tapers to dry. Any leftover wax can be stored in a plastic bag and used to make tapers in moulds (see Amour Tapers).

3. Roll the taper in the tray, allowing any semi-dried bits of wax to stick to the taper in an uneven fashion.

Autumn Melts

This heady combination of essential oils marks the shift from summer to autumn. The warming, spicy aromas from the nutmeg and orange combine with the woody, floral fragrance of the oakmoss and clary sage to create a musky, yet cooling aroma reminiscent of walks through the forest at this atmospheric time of year.

YOU WILL NEED

- 175 g (6 oz) pillar soy wax
- 30 g (1 oz) pillar rapeseed wax
- 3 crushed dried bay leaves
- ice cube tray
- 7 ml (140 drops) orange essential oil
- 2 ml (40 drops) nutmeg essential oil
- 2 ml (40 drops) clary sage essential oil
- 1 ml (20 drops) oakmoss essential oil
- double boiler
- pipettes, for the essential oils
- small container or beaker
- pouring jug (pitcher)

METHOD

1. Crush some dried bay leaves and divide them between the cubes in an ice cube tray.

2. Blend the essential oils together in a small container.

3. Weigh both types of wax and melt them together in the double boiler.

4. Pour 200 ml (7 fl oz) of melted wax into the pouring jug (pitcher). Allow it to stand few a few minutes and then mix in the essential oils.

Pour the wax mixture carefully into the ice cube tray. Leave to set for 24 hours.

5. Tip the melts out of the tray as you would with ordinary ice cubes. Bag them up and tie them with ribbon or raffia for presents. Break up any leftovers in the jug into shards for personal use.

HOW TO USE MELTS

Place the candle melt in the bowl)of your oil burner – there is no need to add water. Light an unscented tealight in the base of the oil burner. The candle melt will gradually turn to liquid wax and will slowly release the essential oil aromas. If you extinguish the tealight, the wax will set and be ready to use again. Keep using the melt until there are no aromas coming from the wax. At this point you will be left with unscented wax – remove the wax by putting the unlit burner in the refrigerator for 15 minutes, which will make the wax shrink away from the sides of the bowl so that you can remove it.

Winter Spice

This candle makes a wonderful present – its spicy, yet fruity aromas will create a warming and cheery atmosphere during the winter months.

YOU WILL NEED

- 200 ml (7 fl oz) capacity glass container
- 200 g (7 oz) container soy wax
- wick, sustainer and wax glue
- splints and elastic bands
- 5 ml (1 tsp) cinnamon essential oil
- 5 ml (1 tsp) orange essential oil
- double boiler
- pipettes, for the essential oils
- small container or beaker
- pouring jug (pitcher)

METHOD

1. Fix the wick to the base of the glass using a blob of wax glue on the sustainer. Make sure the wick is central and fixed into position with the splints and elastic bands, and that it is straight and taut.

2. Weigh 200 g (7 oz) of wax and melt it in the double boiler.

3. Blend the essential oils together in a small container. Pour 200 ml (7 fl oz) into the pouring jug (pitcher), allow it to stand few a few minutes and then mix in the essential oils.

4. Pour the blended wax into the container. As this is a larger container than some of the other projects, it is important to work in a warm atmosphere – this allows the wax to cool slowly and minimizes the chance of the wax cracking on the surface (see troubleshooting notes on page xx).

5. Leave to set for 24 hours, then remove the splints and trim the wick.

Yule Candle

This candle will celebrate this magical time of year with essential oils and perfumes reminiscent of mulled wine, warming fires and good company.

YOU WILL NEED [B]

- 400 ml (14 fl oz) pillar candle mould
- 420 g (15 oz) beeswax
- silicone mould release spray
- square braided wick
- modelling putty
- splints and elastic bands
- 11 ml (220 drops) orange essential oil
- 11 ml (220 drops) cinnamon essential oil
- pipettes, for essential oils
- double boiler
- small container or beaker
- pouring jug (pitcher)
- Tupperware or old ice-cream container, larger than the mould

METHOD

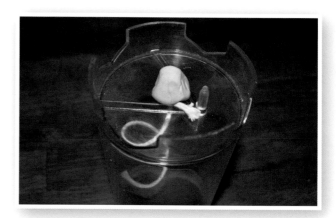

1. Spray the pillar candle mould with a silicone mould release – while this is not essential, it does make the removal of the set candle much easier. Thread the wick through the aperture in the mould and seal with modeling putty. Leave about 7 cm (2¾ in) of the wick on top of the mould (this will be the candle base), as it will give you something to hold on to when pulling the candle out of the mould.

2. Weigh 420 g (15 oz) beeswax and melt it in the double boiler.

3. Mix together the essential oils in a small container. When the wax is fully melted, pour 400ml (14fl oz)into the pouring jug (pitcher) and blend in the essential oils, stirring constantly but trying to avoid creating any air bubbles.

4. Place the mould in a plastic container in case the wax leaks from the receptacle.

5. Pour the blended wax into the mould and allow it to set.

6. Once the wax has set but is still warm to the touch, you should notice that the wax has pulled away from the wick leaving a hole. Re-melt the remaining wax and pour it into the hole to seal the candle base.

7. Leave for 24 hours before pulling the candle out of the mould. If this proves difficult, put the mould into the freezer for an hour and try again.

Christmas Tealights

These tealights are made using glass holders – this gives them a sophisticated styling and also means that they are re-usable. You can, of course, also make them using ordinary moulds. The aromas are spicy, sweet and everything you would expect at this time of year!

YOU WILL NEED

- 8 glass tealight containers
- 200 g (7 oz) container soy wax
- tealight wicks and sustainers
- 4 ml (80 drops) orange essential oil
- 4 ml (80 drops) clove essential oil
- 4 ml (80 drops) cinnamon essential oil
- double boiler
- pipettes, for the essential oils
- small container or beaker
- pouring jug (pitcher)

METHOD

1. Mix together the essential oils in the small container.

2. Weigh 200 g (7 oz) wax for the double boiler. Once melted, pour the wax into the pouring jug (pitcher) and add the essential oil mixture, stirring thoroughly.

Pour the wax mixture into the glass tealight containers and leave for a minute. Place the tealight wicks into the centre of the containers.

3. Leave the tealights to set for 24 hours prior. The wicks are specially designed for tealights so there is no need to trim them. To re-use the containers, remove the old wick remnants and sustainer, wash out any residue wax and start again.

First published in 2015 by New Holland Publishers Pty Ltd
London • Sydney • Auckland

The Chandlery Unit 009 50 Westminster Bridge Road London SE1 7QY United Kingdom
1/66 Gibbes Street Chatswood NSW 2067 Australia
5/39 Woodside Ave Northcote Auckland 0627 New Zealand

www.newhollandpublishers.com

A record of this book is held at the British Library and the National Library of Australia.

ISBN 9781742575766

Managing Director: Fiona Schultz
Production Director: Olga Dementiev
Publisher: Diane Ward
Project Editor: Emma Clegg
Designer: Lorena Susak
Proofreader: Simona Hill
Printer: Toppan Leefung Printing Ltd

10 9 8 7 6 5 4 3 2 1

Keep up with New Holland Publishers on Facebook
www.facebook.com/NewHollandPublishers